Key

to the

Bi-literal Cipher

***of* Francis Bacon**

Key

to the

Bi-literal Cipher

of **Francis Bacon**

By

CHARLES LOUGHRIDGE

DENVER, COLORADO

ISBN: 978-93-5128-845-9(HB)

First Published in 1916
Indian Reprint in 2017

Published by

Kalpaz Publications
C-30, Satyawati Nagar,
Delhi – 110052
E-mail: kalpaz@hotmail.com
Website: kalpazpublications.com
Ph.: +91-9212142040

Cataloging in Publication Data—DK
Courtesy: D.K. Agencies (P) Ltd. <docinfo@dkagencies.com>

Loughridge, Charles, 1858-1928, **author.**
Key to the bi-literal cipher of Francis Bacon / by Charles Loughridge.
pages cm
Reprint. Originally published: 1916.

1. Bacon, Francis, 1561-1626—Cipher. I. Title.

Z103.5.L68 2017 DDC 003.54 23

Key to the

Bi-literal Cipher

of FRANCIS BACON

THE Translation of Biliteral Cipher states that Francis Bacon and the Rev. Wm. Rawley, his Chaplain, Secretary and Literary Executor, kept a diary in a system of shorthand writing, which Bacon invented and named Biliteral Cipher. According to the Cipher Story, the System was devised while Bacon was a youth in Paris, 1576 to 1579. The Alphabets were kept private and secret, until 1623, when standard alphabets and a Key Example were made known by publication in De Augmentis Scientiarum.

An Example of a Bi-literal Alphabet

A	B	C	D	E	F
aaaaa	aaaab.	aaaba.	aaabb.	aabaa.	aabab.
G	H	I	K	L	M
aabba	aabbb.	abaaa.	abaab.	ababa.	ababb.
N	O	P	Q	R	S
abbaa.	abbab.	abbba.	abbbb.	baaaa.	baaab.
T	V	W	X	Y	Z
baaba.	baabb.	babaa.	babab.	babba.	babbb.

Example of Solution

F	U	G	E
aabab	baabb	aabba	aabaa

To gain secrecy and allay curiosity, the Example of Solution:

aababbaabbaabbaaabaa,

was resolved, by printing, into Bi-formed fonts of Script letters. The letters were engraved from letters in a special Bi-formed Alphabet, which was designed by Francis Bacon and is reproduced in facsimile as follows:

An Example of a Bi-formed Alphabet

Ego omni officio, ac potius pietate erga te· caeteris satisfacio omnibus: Mihi ipse nunquàm satisfacio. Tanta est enim magnitudo tuorum erga me meritorum, vt quoniam tu, nisi perfectâ re, de me non conquiêsti; ego, quia non idem in tuâ causâ efficio, vitam mihi esse acerbam putem. In causâ haec sunt: Ammonius Regis legatus apertè pecuniâ nos oppugnat. Res agitur per eosdem creditores, per quos, cùm tu aderas, agebatur. Regis causâ, si qui sunt, qui velint, qui pauci sunt, omnes ad Pompeium rem deferri volunt. Senatus Religionis calumniam, non religione, sed malevolentia, et illius Regiae Largitionis inuidiâ comprobat. &c.

Bacon prepared an ample Example of Biliteral Cipher, Omnia per Omnia, i. e., using the entire text of the exterior or infolding letter.

The hidden, interior or infolded message is a Spartan Letter which was sent once in a Scytale or round cipher staff.

Perditae res. Mindarus cecidit. Milites Esuriunt. Neque hinc nos extricare, neque hic diutiús manere possumus.

Bacon ciphered the Spartan Letter in Biliteral Cipher, in a part of Cicero's Epistle, as the Standard or Key-Example. The Letter was first ciphered into the Bi-literal Alphabet, as in the Example of Solution. Next, the Example of Solution was resolved or ciphered into the engraved letters of the Epistle, employing the Bi-formed Script Alphabet shown in the foregoing Epistle of Cicero.

The engraver varied slightly from some of the designs of the Standard Bi-formed Alphabet. The variations may be a masque to make it harder to understand the Cipher.

Bacon's use of Bi-literal Cipher remained an undisclosed secret until 1895, when it was discovered and made public by Mrs. Elizabeth Wells Gallup.

By a stroke of genius, Mrs. Gallup evolved from the Standard Alphabets and Key-Examples, a system of design and rules on which to assemble Bi-formed Alphabets for use in deciphering.

A Bi-formed Alphabet is required for each new Work and for each font of Italics. The Italic type used are cut from Bi-formed Alphabets designed by the cipherer. The type which were used in printing the Italics in Novum Organum 1620, Henry VII 1622, De Augmentis 1623, and Shakespeare were cut after designs made by Bacon. The standard of design is embodied in the Bi-formed Alphabet, given in De Augmentis Scientiarum.

Everyone should learn the modus operandi or mechanism of Biliteral Cipher. Few, not to exceed ten, have done original deciphering. All can use to advantage the narrative revealed by the Translations now made.

The Biliteral Alphabet, the Bi-formed Alphabet and the Key-Example were published at London in 1623, contemporaneously with The First Folio of Shakespeare.

The publication in 1623 was in the London Edition of De Augmentis Scientiarum; in 1624, in the Paris Edition; in London, in the Latin Edition of 1638; and at London in the English Edition 1640. The Alphabets in each are substantially the same. The differences may result from the engraver's variations or from tricks native to the Art of Cyphers.

To decipher the Spartan Letter, read the font of each letter. Mark one font as "a"; the other, as "b". In the Key to the Fonts, a-font is indicated by a small Roman letter and b-font, by a Capital letter. Consult a printer, if the font rule is not clear.

The transcription is elaborately worked out in the Treatise by Mrs. Fiske entitled, "Studies in the Biliteral Cipher of Francis Bacon," published by John W. Luce & Co. of Boston.

Key to the Fonts of the Letters in Cicero's Epistle

eGOOm niOff Icioa cpoTI uSpie TatEe rgate caEte Rissa tiSfa CiocoM nlbUS mIhii pSEnu nquAM satis Facio TanTA EsteN immAg niTud otuOr uMerg ameME rItor UmvTq uOnIA mTuni sIpEr fEcta RedEm enOnc Onqul esTie Goqul AnoNI Demin tUaca UsaEF fICio VitAm mIHie ssEac eRBAM PutEM inCau saHAE cSunt aMMon iusRe gISle gATuS AperT apEcu NiAnO SopPu Gnatr eSagi turPe recsd Emcre diTor eSPer quOsc uMTUA DerAS agEba tuRRE gIsca UsasI quiSU nTqui VelIN TquIp aUcis UntOM NesaD pOmPE inmre mDEfe rrIvo Lunts enAtu sRELi glOnI ScalU MniaM NonRE lIgIO NesED MaleU oLENt iaEtI lLius ReGia elarg ition isinu idiac ompro bat etc. etc.

Note—Resolve each Symbol into terms of the Biliteral Alphabet, thus: eGOOm reads abbba, which is the Symbol for P.; niOff=aabaa=E; Icioa=baaaa=r and so on to the end. Such resolutions produce the Spartan Letter.

Perditae Res Mindarus cecidit. Milites esuriunt. Neque hinc nos extricare neque his diutius manere possumus.

The discovery of how to assemble a Bi-formed Alphabet to decipher with, is a work of first magnitude. The rules are fully explained in the Work by Mrs. Fiske. The Key-Alphabets and Examples were preserved in letters of Script design as a mask. Other masks are used in the context in De Augmentis and in The

Example itself to make it difficult to decipher and to conceal Bacon's use of the Cipher.

"Far fro' th' nest" the Lapwing crys, "away."

Mrs. Gallup deciphered the narrative in the Italic letters of The Advancement of Learning 1605, Shepheards Calenders 1579, King Henry VII 1622, The Folio of Shakespeare 1623, and other Works. The translation was published in 1899 for private circulation.

Mrs. Gallup, assisted by Miss Kate E. Wells, continued the work of transcription. Many rare volumes were deciphered, in the Libraries of London, New York and Boston. The narrative translated from some sixty volumes dating between 1579 and 1671 was published in 1910 as "The Biliteral Cipher of Francis Bacon."

The main function of Biliteral Cipher is to teach Word Cipher and to preserve aids, rules and instructions for use in writing it. A brief autobiography of Francis Bacon and comments on contemporaries are also preserved in it.

The translation is a Work which is monumental in character. It may be termed the Rosetta stone of English; for it reveals elements and methods of expression which herald the dawning of a Second Golden Age of English thought and language.

Under the magic influence, Shakespeare becomes more understandable than ever. The information revealed unlocks and explains, with surpassing interest, many of the dark and unfathomed things in Shakespeare and Elizabethan Literature.

Table of Works Deciphered

The narrative translated is published as "The Biliteral Cipher of Francis Bacon," "Lost Manuscripts" and "Studies in the Biliteral Cipher of Francis Bacon."

The narrative deciphered was ciphered in Biliteral Cipher in the Italic letters of the works named as follows:

Shepheard's Calendar	1579	Anonymous
The Arraignment of Paris	1584	George Peele
The Mirrour of Modestie	1584	Robert Greene
Planetomachia	1585	Robert Greene
A Treatise on Melancholy	1586	T. Bright
Euphues Morando	1587	Robert Greene
Spanish Masquerado	1589	Robert Greene
Complaints	1591	Edmund Spenser
Colin Clout	1595	Edmund Spenser
Faerie Queene	1596	Edmund Spenser
Faerie Queene (second part)		Edmund Spenser
Richard II	1598	Anonymous
David & Bethsabe	1599	George Peele
Knight of the Golden Shield	1599	George Peele
Midsummer Night's Dream	1600	Wm. Shakespeare
Midsummer Night's Dream (Fisher Edition)		Wm. Shakespeare
Much Ado About Nothing	1600	Wm. Shakespeare
Sir John Oldcastle	1600	Wm. Shakespeare
Richard, Duke of York	1600	Wm. Shakespeare
Treasons of Essex	1601	Francis Bacon
London Prodigal	1605	Wm. Shakespeare
Advancement of Learning	1605	Francis Bacon
King Lear	1608	Wm. Shakespeare
Henry V	1608	Wm. Shakespeare
Pericles	1609	Wm. Shakespeare
Hamlet	1611	Wm. Shakespeare
Titus Andronicus	1611	Wm. Shakespeare
Shepheard's Calendar	1611	Edmund Spenser
Faerie Queene	1613	Edmund Spenser
Richard II	1615	Wm. Shakespeare
Plays in Folio	1616	Ben Jonson
Merry Wives of Windsor	1619	Wm. Shakespeare
Contention of York	1619	Wm. Shakespeare
Pericles	1619	Wm. Shakespeare
Yorkshire Tragedy	1619	Wm. Shakespeare
Romeo and Juliet	No date	Wm. Shakespeare
A Quit for an Upstart	1620	Robert Greene
Novum Organum	1620	Francis Bacon
The Parasceve	1620	Francis Bacon
Henry VII	1622	Francis Bacon
Edward II	1622	Christopher Marlowe
Historia Vitae et Mortes	1623	Francis Bacon
Historia Ventorum	1622	Francis Bacon
Folio of Shakespeare	1623	Wm. Shakespeare
De Augmentis Scientiarum	1623	Francis Bacon
De Augmentis Scientiarum	1624	Francis Bacon
Apophthegmes	1625	Francis Bacon
Essays	1625	Francis Bacon
Sylva Sylvarum	1627	Francis Bacon
Anatomy of Melancholy	1628	Robert Burton
The Miscellany	1629	Wm. Rawley
Folio of Shakespeare	1632	Wm. Shakespeare
New Atlantis	1635	Francis Bacon
Sylva Sylvarum	1635	Francis Bacon
Felicity of Queen Elizabeth	1657	Wm. Rawley
Resuscitatio	1657	Wm. Rawley
Resuscitatio	1671	Wm. Dugdale